Candace Parker

THE STORY OF THE CHICAGO SKY

T0019662

Kahleah Copper

WNBA: A HISTORY OF WOMEN'S HOOPS

THE STORY OF THE

CHICAGO SKY

JIM WHITING

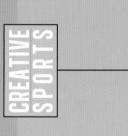

Cappie Pondexter

CREATIVE EDUCATION / CREATIVE PAPERBACKS

Published by Creative Education and Creative Paperbacks
P.O. Box 227, Mankato, Minnesota 56002
Creative Education and Creative Paperbacks are imprints of
The Creative Company
www.thecreativecompany.us

Design and production by Blue Design (www.bluedes.com)
Art direction by Rita Marshall

Photographs by AP Images (Jeff Roberson), Getty (Icon Sportswire, Ethan
Miller, Michael Reaves, Jennifer Stewart)

Library of Congress Cataloging-in-Publication Data
Names: Whiting, Jim, 1943- author.
Title: The story of the Chicago Sky / by Jim Whiting.
Description: Mankato, Minnesota : Creative Education and Creative
    Paperbacks, [2024] | Series: Creative Sports. WNBA : A History of
    Women's Hoops. | Includes index. | Audience: Ages 8-12 | Audience:
    Grades 4-6 | Summary: "Middle grade basketball fans are introduced to
    the extraordinary history of WNBA's Chicago Sky with a photo-laden
    narrative of their greatest successes and losses"-- Provided by
    publisher.
Identifiers: LCCN 2022034234 (print) | LCCN 2022034235 (ebook) | ISBN
    9781640267176 (library binding) | ISBN 9781682772737 (paperback) | ISBN
    9781640008687 (pdf)
Subjects: LCSH: Chicago Sky (Basketball team)--History--Juvenile
    literature.
Classification: LCC GV885.52.C47 W55 2023 (print) | LCC GV885.52.C47
    (ebook) | DDC 796.323/640977311--dc23/eng/20220720
LC record available at https://lccn.loc.gov/2022034234
LC ebook record available at https://lccn.loc.gov/2022034235

Printed in China

Allie Quigley

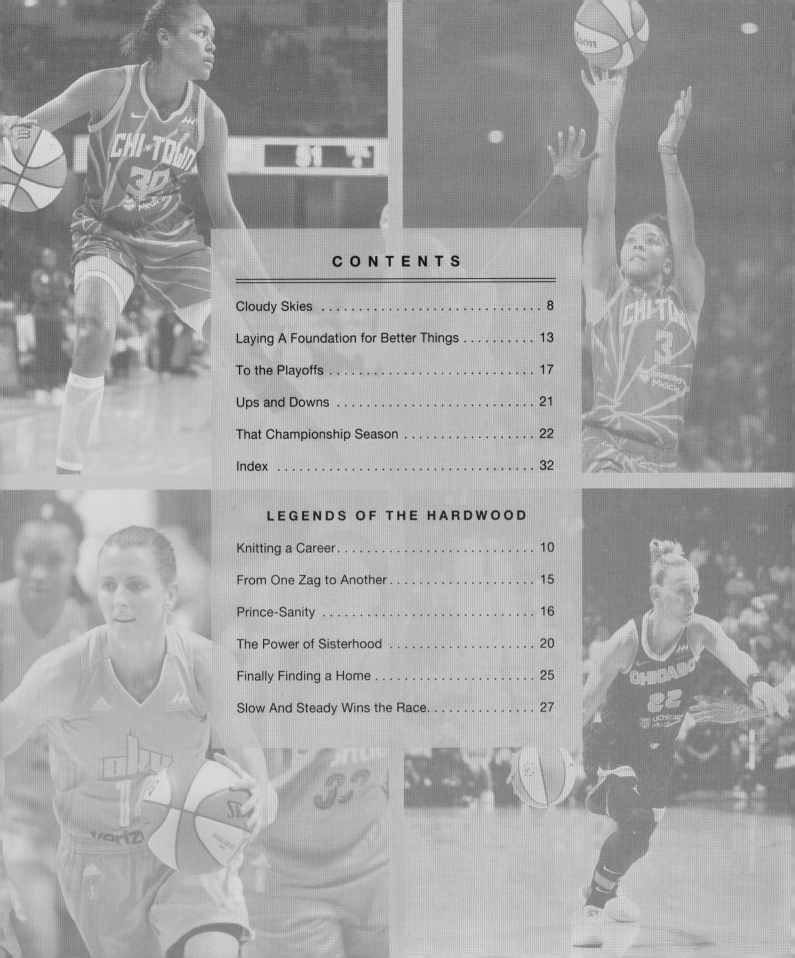

CONTENTS

LEGENDS OF THE HARDWOOD

CLOUDY SKIES

The Chicago Sky seemed well on their way to winning their first-ever game in the Women's National Basketball Association (WNBA) on May 20, 2006. They led the Charlotte Sting by 16 points. Just three minutes remained to play. At that point, though, Charlotte stung the Sky with 18 unanswered points. They surged ahead 82–80. Less than four seconds remained. "For 35 minutes, we played great," Chicago coach Dave Cowens said. "Then we stopped scoring. I can't explain it—we just couldn't score." Chicago guard Jia Perkins—who had played for Charlotte for two seasons before coming to Chicago—put up a desperation three-point attempt with one second left. It missed, badly. But Charlotte made one of the worst mistakes in basketball. They fouled a three-point shooter with time almost expired. Perkins sank all three free throws. Chicago had its first win, 83–82.

For one game, at least, the Sky lived up to their nickname. As team president Margaret Stender explained, the name symbolized "a beautiful day in Chicago

Jia Perkins

LEGENDS OF THE HARDWOOD

SYLVIA FOWLES
CENTER
HEIGHT: 6-FOOT-6
SKY SEASONS: 2008–14

Sylvia Fowles

KNITTING A CAREER

As a youngster, Sylvia Fowles ran track and played volleyball. She was also interested in "home arts," such as sewing and cooking. She finally began playing basketball in the eighth grade. Sometimes she played in games against her brother. He encouraged his teammates to knock her down. That helped toughen her. She had a sensational high school career. In 2001, she became the first female high schooler to dunk. She was named a McDonald's All-American. Fowles didn't leave her past behind when she visited Louisiana State University on a recruiting visit. She knitted a sweater for one of the coaches. She led the Tigers to three NCAA Final Four appearances. With the Sky, she was named to the All-WNBA team four times and played in three All-Star Games.

between the blue sky and bright sunlight to highlight the spectacular skyline."

But there weren't many "beautiful days" in the rest of the season. Chicago had just four other wins. Their 5–29 record was one of the worst in WNBA history. They were last in the WNBA's Eastern Conference. One reason was that Chicago was an expansion team. They got to choose one player from every other WNBA team. Those teams protected their best players. So, most of Chicago's choices were role players. They weren't used to playing for long periods of time. The Sky did have the sixth overall pick in the 2006 WNBA Draft before the season. They took power forward Candice Dupree. She averaged 13.7 points and 5.5 rebounds per game. She was named to the All-Star Game and the WNBA All-Rookie First Team.

The Sky played much better in 2007. They matched the previous season's win total by their 10th game. They exceeded it in the following game to go 6–5. But they won only two of the next eight games. They finished 14–20. Again they were last in the Eastern Conference. One bright spot was rookie guard Armintie Price (name later changed to Price-Herrington). She had been the third overall choice in the 2007 WNBA Draft. She started every game and averaged nearly eight points, six rebounds, and three assists per game. She also played solid defense. She was named WNBA Rookie of the Year. Dupree was an All-Star for the second time.

After splitting their first two games in 2008, the Sky lost their next three games. They never got back to the .500 level. They finished 12–22 and were fifth in the conference. Center Sylvia Fowles had been the second overall pick in the 2008 WNBA Draft. She averaged nearly 11 points and more than 7 rebounds per game. She was named to the All-Rookie First Team. But she was injured and played in just half of the team's games.

LAYING A FOUNDATION FOR BETTER THINGS

The Sky began the 2009 season with six wins in the first nine games. Fans hoped the team would record its first winning season. That hope continued through mid-August. Chicago was 13–12 at that point. But the Sky won just three of their next nine games. They finished 16–18. Dupree, Perkins, and Fowles were named to the All-Star Game.

The Sky were looking for their first winning season in 2010. They were at .500 24 games in, but that was the high-water mark of the season. Chicago lost the next five games. They went on to finish 14–20. Fowles was finally healthy for the entire season. She set a team record with 606 points. Guard Epiphanny Prince was named to the WNBA All-Rookie First Team.

During the early part of the 2011 season, the Sky struggled to surpass the .500 mark. They finally reached it at 8–8 but couldn't sustain the momentum. They finished 14–20 for the second season in a row. Chicago drafted point guard Courtney Vandersloot with the third overall pick in the 2011 WNBA Draft. She had been the first college player—male or female—with 2,000 points and 1,000 assists in her career. She lived up to the hype by being named to the WNBA All-Rookie First Team and the All-Star Game. Fowles finished the season as only the

Courtney Vandersloot

second player in league history to average at least 20 points and 10 rebounds per game. She was also named the WNBA Defensive Player of the Year.

Chicago opened the 2012 season with seven wins in the first eight games. But they won just one of the next nine to drop to 8–9 before the six-week Olympics break. They lost five more when play resumed. The Sky split the remaining 12 games to finish 14–20 for the third year in a row.

Sylvia Fowles

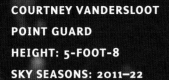

COURTNEY VANDERSLOOT
POINT GUARD
HEIGHT: 5-FOOT-8
SKY SEASONS: 2011–22

FROM ONE ZAG TO ANOTHER

Courtney Vandersloot was Washington State's high school player of the year in 2007. Her coach at Gonzaga University suggested that she call Hall of Fame point guard John Stockton for advice on playing the position. He had been a star at Gonzaga and went on to set the all-time NBA record for assists. "It was just the opportunity of a lifetime," she said. "He has that knowledge he can share. The things he does are all based on confidence." He passed that confidence on to Vandersloot. She became a three-time college All-American. She has had an outstanding career with the Sky. She was twice named to the All-WNBA First Team, is a three-time All-Star, and holds several WNBA assists records. "She is the female John Stockton," said former teammate Katelan Redmon.

Epiphanny Prince

EPIPHANNY PRINCE
GUARD
HEIGHT: 5-FOOT-9
SKY SEASONS:
2010-14

PRINCE-SANITY

In 2011, Jeremy Lin of the New York Knicks led his team on a hot seven-game winning streak. He ignited a nationwide craze called "Linsanity," a combination of his last name and "insanity." The Sky had its own version in 2012. They opened the season with two wins in the first three games. Then they won six in a row. The primary reason for the win streak was guard Epiphanny Prince. She had three consecutive games of at least 30 points. That tied a league record. All three games led to come-from-behind victories. Twice Prince sank last-second shots to send games into overtime. Her exploits were named "Prince-sanity." She put up big numbers for several more games, until she broke her foot. At the time, she was leading the league with an average of 24.3 points per game.

TO THE PLAYOFFS

The Sky won four of their first seven games in 2013. Chicago romped through the rest of the schedule. Their 24–10 record was seven games better than any other team in the Eastern Conference. One key factor was small forward/shooting guard Elena Delle Donne. She had been named one of the WNBA's "Three to See" campaign before the season. It featured three highly rated rookies. She proved that the league was right. She averaged more than 18 points and 5 rebounds per game. She was the first rookie to be the leading vote-getter for the All-Star Game. Delle Donne was also only the second player to earn the WNBA Rookie of the Month award all five times.

Chicago had their first winning record. It was also their first playoff berth. The Sky faced the Indiana Fever in the Eastern Conference semifinals. It wasn't an ideal matchup. The Fever had handed the Sky three of their regular-season losses. Indiana swept the best-of-three series.

The Sky fell back to a losing record in 2014. Fowles, Delle Donne, and Vandersloot all missed much of the season. After starting 4–0, Chicago finished 15–19. That record was still good enough for the playoffs. The Sky faced the Atlanta Dream in the conference semifinals. They were back to full strength. Vandersloot hit a game-winning 20-foot jump shot with 20 seconds left in Game 1. Atlanta evened the series in Game 2.

Game 3 was a classic. The Dream led 67–51 at the end of the third quarter. Delle Donne exploded for 17 points in the fourth quarter. She sank the game-winning shot over two defenders with 8.4 seconds remaining. Chicago won 81–80. It is the biggest fourth-quarter comeback in WNBA playoff history. "In the fourth quarter, coach put the ball in my hands, the team trusted me and it just went from there," Delle Donne said. "So I was very confident."

That set up a rematch with the Fever in the best-of-three conference finals. Indiana won the first game. The Fever led Game 2 by two points in the closing seconds. Then the Sky's small forward Tamera Young tipped in a missed shot to tie the score with one second remaining, forcing overtime. The score remained tied at the end of overtime. That forced a second overtime. Chicago won 86–84. The Sky went on to win Game 3, 75–62, and advanced to their first WNBA Finals.

Chicago faced Phoenix for the WNBA title. The Mercury had won 29 games. That is the most in WNBA history. Phoenix routed Chicago in the first two games of the best-of-five series, 83–62 and 97–68, respectively. The Sky battled back in Game 3. They led 63–61 after three quarters. Mercury star Diana Taurasi's three-point play with 14 seconds left broke an 82–82 fourth-quarter tie. Phoenix won 87–82.

Chicago went 21–13 in 2015. Delle Donne had a career game against the Dream on June 24. She scored 45 points and blocked six shots. Her 19 made free throws were the third highest in league history. She became the first Chicago player named league Most Valuable Player (MVP). The Sky faced the Fever in the conference semifinals. Chicago won Game 1, 77–72. Indiana won the next two to take the series.

Cappie Pondexter

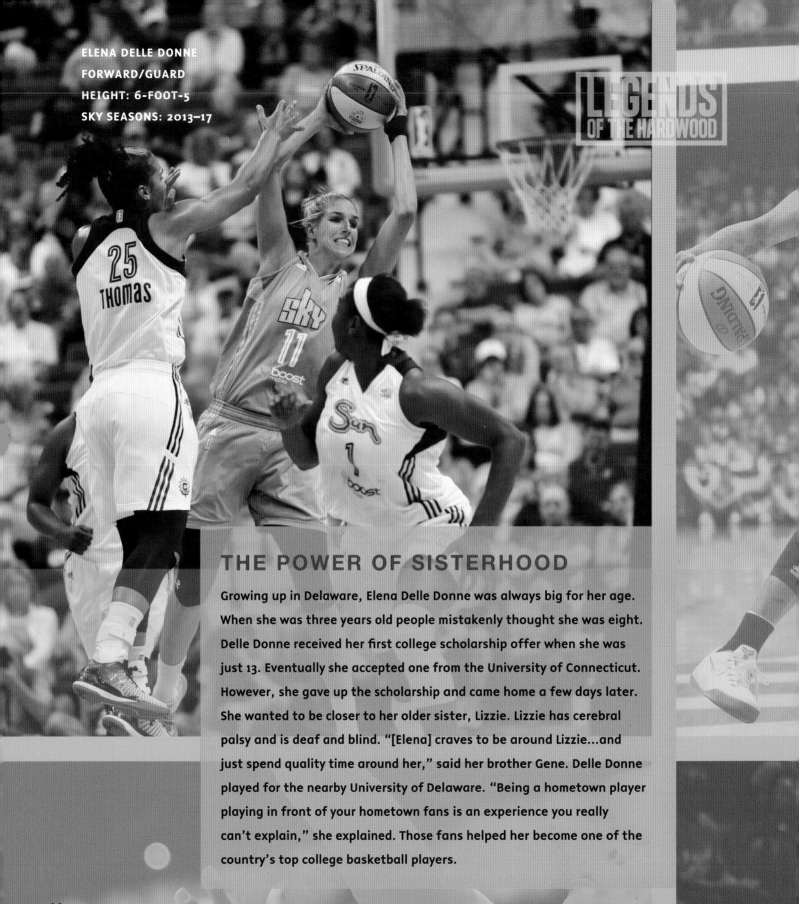

ELENA DELLE DONNE
FORWARD/GUARD
HEIGHT: 6-FOOT-5
SKY SEASONS: 2013–17

THE POWER OF SISTERHOOD

Growing up in Delaware, Elena Delle Donne was always big for her age. When she was three years old people mistakenly thought she was eight. Delle Donne received her first college scholarship offer when she was just 13. Eventually she accepted one from the University of Connecticut. However, she gave up the scholarship and came home a few days later. She wanted to be closer to her older sister, Lizzie. Lizzie has cerebral palsy and is deaf and blind. "[Elena] craves to be around Lizzie...and just spend quality time around her," said her brother Gene. Delle Donne played for the nearby University of Delaware. "Being a hometown player playing in front of your hometown fans is an experience you really can't explain," she explained. Those fans helped her become one of the country's top college basketball players.

UPS AND DOWNS

By mid-July of the 2016 season, the Sky were just 8–12. They won seven of the next eight games to raise their record to 15–13. They split the remaining six games to finish 18–16. It was the fourth-best mark in the league. The WNBA had changed its playoff format. The eight teams with the best overall records qualified, regardless of their conference. The first two rounds consisted of single games involving the teams seeded three through eight.

Chicago had a first-round bye. The Sky defeated the Dream 108–98 in the second round. They faced the Los Angeles Sparks in the best-of-five league semifinals. Los Angeles easily won the first two games. Chicago narrowly won Game 3, 70–66. The Sparks opened up a 55–33 halftime lead in Game 4. They cruised to a 95–75 victory to win the series.

The 2017 season was disappointing. The Sky traded Delle Donne. Without her, Chicago began with just one win in their first seven games. They won only two more in the next eight. The Sky did play a little better the rest of the way. They won 9 of the final 19 games to finish 12–22. They were far from playoff contention.

The 2018 season was a virtual duplicate of the previous one. After a 3–3 start, the Sky lost the next six. They never came close to a winning record. They finished 13–21.

It was a different story in 2019. Chicago began the season 6–3. They fell to 7–8 in mid-July but won seven of the next eight games. Their final record was 20–14. That gave them the fifth seed in the playoffs. In the first round, they broke open a tight game against Phoenix in the third quarter and crushed the Mercury, 105–76. Diamond DeShields scored 25 points for Chicago. Four of her teammates also scored in double figures. The Sky led the Las Vegas Aces by two points near the end of the second-round game. They tried to run out the final moments. Dearica Hamby of the Aces stole an errant pass with nine seconds remaining. She misread the clock and heaved a desperate three-point shot. It went in and gave the Aces a 93–92 victory.

THAT CHAMPIONSHIP SEASON

Chicago hoped to build on the momentum of the 2019 season in 2020. But the COVID-19 pandemic hit. The season was played entirely in Bradenton, Florida, without fans. It began several weeks later than originally planned and was reduced to 22 games. Chicago got off to a 10–4 start. Several injuries reduced their final mark to 12–10. They lost in the first round of the playoffs to the Connecticut Sun, 94–81.

The team made one key addition before the 2021 season. Forward/center Candace Parker returned to her native Chicago after 13 years starring for the Los Angeles Sparks. "Winning a championship back home would mean so much," she explained. Title thoughts seemed to dim when the Sky lost seven of their first nine games. Then a seven-game winning streak raised their record to 9–7. They finished 16–16. That gave them the sixth seed in the playoffs. They easily defeated the Dallas Wings in the first round, 81–64. They knocked off the Minnesota Lynx in the second round, 89–76.

Candace Parker

ALLIE QUIGLEY
GUARD
HEIGHT: 5-FOOT-10
SKY SEASONS:
2013-PRESENT

FINALLY FINDING A HOME

The Seattle Storm drafted Allie Quigley in 2008. She was cut during training camp. She then signed with the Phoenix Mercury. But they cut her early in the 2009 season. She played briefly with the Indiana Fever and San Antonio Silver Stars in 2010. She tried again with Seattle in 2011. She scored four points in seven games. She was cut yet again. She didn't play at all in 2012. Instead, she worked as a basketball camp counselor. She thought her WNBA career was over. Chicago offered her a chance in 2013. She played in all 34 games. The following year, she was named the WNBA Sixth Woman of the Year. That honors a player who comes off the bench to provide scoring punch. Since then, she has played in three All-Star Games. "It feels awesome just to know that all these ups and downs over the years and hard work has paid off," Quigley said.

CHICAGO SKY

The Sky faced Connecticut in the semifinals. The Sun's 26 wins were the most in the WNBA that season. The teams split the first two games in the best-of-five series. With seven minutes left in Game 3, the Sun led 72–65. Three minutes later, the Sky took a 75–74 lead on a layup by forward Azurá Stevens. They gradually extended it to six points. With 42 seconds remaining, Connecticut cut the lead to one at 84–83. Vandersloot was fouled and had two free throws with eight seconds left. She sank one for a two-point lead. Connecticut missed two lay-ins. They fouled Parker with two seconds remaining. Her free throw gave Chicago an 86–83 win. The Sky closed out the best-of-five series with a 79–69 victory in Game 4.

Chicago faced the Mercury for the WNBA title. It was only the second time the Sky had advanced this far. They easily won the first game in the best-of-five series, 91–77. Chicago had a six-point lead at the start of the fourth quarter of Game 2. The game went to overtime. Phoenix pulled out a 91–86 win.

The Sky bounced back to crush the Mercury in Game 3, 86–50. Vandersloot knocked down 26 points, and Kahleah Copper added 24. Phoenix took a 65–54 lead into the fourth quarter of Game 4. Chicago tied it at 72–72 with just under two minutes remaining. Center Stefanie Dolson had two lay-ins in the next minute to give the Sky a 76–72 lead. Vandersloot's two free throws with 10 seconds left iced the game. Chicago won 80–74. They were the WNBA champions for the first time! Vandersloot had 15 assists. That is the second-highest single-game total in WNBA playoff history. Copper averaged 17 points and 5.5 rebounds a game during the series. She was named the Finals MVP. "Everything that this team went through the entire year prepared us for this," Parker said. "We were down 9, we

KAHLEAH COPPER
FORWARD/GUARD
HEIGHT: 6-FOOT-1
SKY SEASONS:
2017-PRESENT

SLOW AND STEADY WINS THE RACE

Kahleah Copper isn't from Philadelphia. She's from *North* Philly, she tells people. That area is known for its gritty lifestyle and hustle. Copper honed her game on the neighborhood streets. She played against older and stronger boys. The lessons paid off. Copper was a McDonald's All-American in high school. She had an outstanding college career at Rutgers University. She was the seventh overall pick in the 2016 WNBA Draft by the Washington Mystics. She averaged just six points a game as a rookie. She was traded to Chicago. In 2020, she became a starter. Her scoring average per game zoomed to 14.9. She was named to the All-Star Game the following season. She played a key role as the Sky won the WNBA title. She was named the Finals MVP.

CHICAGO SKY

Azurá Stevens

were down 11. We just got to stay with it, and that's what we've done all season. I am so proud of this group, with our fight, next-man-up mentality."

After starting 4–3 in 2022, Chicago had winning streaks of five and then six games to notch a 21–6 mark as the season wound down. They finished 26–10 to match the Las Vegas Aces for the league's best record. It was also the best record in team history. The Sky hoped to become the first team since the Los Angeles Sparks in 2001–02 to win two titles in a row.

They lost the first game in the best-of-three first-round series to the New York Liberty. Chicago roared back to win Game 2, 100–62. The 38-point difference is the largest in WNBA playoff history. The Sky easily won Game 3 to face the Connecticut Sun in the best-of-five semifinals. Chicago had defeated the Sun in all four meetings during the season.

Chicago won two of the first three games. Connecticut won Game 4 to force a decisive fifth game. Chicago led by 10 points after three quarters. But with 4:46 remaining, and still holding a nine-point edge, the lid of their basket slammed shut. They went scoreless the rest of the way. Connecticut scored the game's final 18 points to emerge with a 72–63 win. Chicago's total of just five points in the final quarter was the lowest in franchise history. "We just couldn't get a basket," said coach James Wade. "It was tough for us to navigate around them and get to the lane . . . It's probably one of the biggest disappointments that I've had professionally."

The Chicago Sky has tasted both the highs and lows of the WNBA. They began with one of the league's worst all-time records in their first season and rose to the title in 2021. Fans hope that coming years will add more championships.

Candace Parker

INDEX